Yesterday's Child

Fond memories of my grandparents' farm

Published by
HenschelHAUS Publishing, Inc.
www.henschelHAUSbooks.com
Milwaukee, Wisconsin

ISBN: 9798990820364
LCCN: 2024946858

Cover art: *Girl on a Tire Swing*
By Patricia L. Jones

Printed in the USA

*Patricia, thanks for sending me
on a beautiful writing journey.*

Table of Contents

Foreword

Rose Bingham has written an easy-to-read, detail-rich, story of her memories, as a little girl during the years 1940 to 1947, of her Polish grandparents' farm, You will learn about a Midwestern farmstead—the buildings that made it up, especially the farmhouse. You will sit in on a Polish songfest, something that occurred regularly on Saturday nights at her grandparents' farmhouse. You'll read about how Rose's mother and grandmother took little Rose outside on a dark night to look at the stars, and appreciate the night sky. You'll go with Rose to the local feed mill and smell the earthy smell of ground grain.

What was fun on a farm during the 1940s, before TV and cell phones? You'll learn it here. For example, an old tire swing hanging in a tree provided hours of entertainment. You'll go with little Rose to the Juneau County fair and ride the Tilt-a-Whirl, the merry-go-round, and real Shetland ponies.

Rose Bingham has done an excellent job of capturing what Midwestern farm life was like when she was a little girl. Read the book—you'll learn much, and besides you'll enjoy doing it.

—Jerry Apps
Author of several books on early farm life, and seven PBS hour-long TV documentaries.

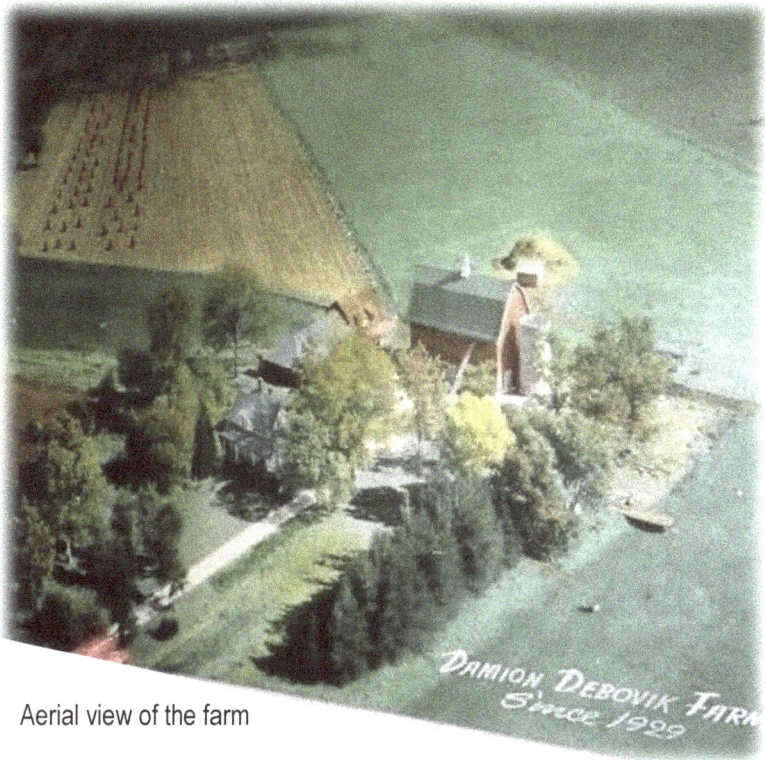

Aerial view of the farm

Childhood Memories of the Farm

I am cuddling up under a feather-tick comforter, waking up to the crowing of a rooster and the smell of fresh baked bread.

I am a little girl in bib overalls, hair in pigtails, walking into the barn, watching kittens lapping milk, Holsteins swishing tails, and hearing the horses gently snorting air through their nostrils.

I am priming the water pump, hearing the squeak, squeak of the handle, bending down and peering into the spout, delighted when water appears, first a trickle and then a gush.

I am walking through the barnyard, listening to a chorus of pigs oinking, chickens clucking, and cows mooing.

I am waving to Grampa who I see out in the field behind the plow.

I am stopping for a ride on my tire swing, rotating my feet until the rope is taut, lifting my feet off the ground and spinning wildly.

I am strolling through the orchard anticipating the harvest of apples and cherries.

I am walking past the front porch lined with
lace curtains drying on stretchers.

I am stopping to sit a moment at the edge of
the pond, delighted to see a goldfish peeking
around a lily pad.

I am going into the cellar, a special place,
with potatoes and carrots in the bins,
sauerkraut curing in a crock, fruit jars on
the shelf making a rainbow of color.

I am playing Chinese checkers with
Grandma, the aroma of tea brewing on the
potbelly stove, the end of a perfect day.

Introduction

I received the following text in 2023 from my sister, Patricia.

> *"Rose, I have no Memories, so I would Love any stories You would like to share. Have fun!! This will be so Great!!"*

She wanted me to share what I remembered about our maternal grandparents' farm life. Being the oldest, I was fortunate to have Grandma in my world for ten years, 1937 to 1947. Patricia was born in 1949, two years after Grandma died from a stroke. Grampa's son, Tony, helped him run the farm for a few years after Grandma died, but then the farm was sold and he lived with a daughter in Chicago, Illinois. Grampa died years later in 1968.

Patricia gave me a wooden stand-up plaque that sits atop my computer desk: ***Love, which makes life more beautiful and story worth telling***. Patricia, thanks for asking me to do this. My hope is you, our family, and my readers will enjoy a bit of nostalgia of days gone by.

The wisdom of age reveals the treasures of youth. My treasures are fond memories of my maternal grandparents in rural Mauston, Wisconsin, and lessons I learned.

My story really begins when Fred Steinmetz accepted employment as a hired hand on the farm of Marian and Damian Debovik in 1935 and fell in love with their daughter, Eleanor. Eleanor and Fred married August 29,1936 and welcomed me into the world on July19,1937.

* * *

Marian Stuczynski was born August 16, 1882, in Plock, Poland, and came to the United States at the age of eight. Damian Cosmas Debovik was born November 14, 1883 in Grodno, Belarus, and came to the United States at the age of twenty-one. Their paths would cross when she, Marian Stuczynski Czajka, was a

Grandma and Grampa Debovik

8

supervisor, rare in those days, at Argo Starch Company in Summit, Illinois, which the locals called Argo.

Damian Debovik worked at the plant and had great respect for her. Marian's husband, John Czajka, died December 25, 1910, leaving her with six children: Frank, John, Clara, Regina, Anthony, and Martha. When Marian became ill and

Back row, L to R: John Czajka, Anthony Czajka, Grandma Devovik, Frank Czajka, Grandpa Devovic
2nd row: Martha Czajka, Clara Czajka, Regina Czajka
Front row: Eleanor and Isabel Devovik

The house in Germantown.

The farmhouse in rural Mauston, WI.

required hospitalization, the authorities wanted to place her children in foster homes. Damian came to the hospital and said, "I don't know if you could learn to love me, but I will marry you to help with your children." She agreed.

They married November 23, 1912, at St. Joseph Catholic Church in Summit, Illinois. It was a match made in heaven and they had two children of their own, Isabel, September 14, 1913, and our mother, Eleanor, November 14, 1915.

I'm uncertain as to when they relocated from Summit, Illinois to Wisconsin but sometime in the early 1920s. They first moved to Germantown in Juneau County situated at the junction of the Wisconsin and Yellow rivers and had to leave because of flooding. According to www.townof-germantown.com, I ascertained it was intentional flooding.

The plans for the two lakes and dams were initiated in the late 1920s by the Wisconsin River Power Company.

The buildings in Germantown were disassembled and used for houses in Mauston and the area became the Castle Rock County Park. The site of Werner was submerged beneath the waters of the lake. The same lake waters that submerged its

11

early beginnings have, in recent years, led to the remarkable growth that the town is experiencing. The Castle Rock and Petenwell lakes and dams, completed in 1950, opened up a new era for both Juneau and Adams counties.

As a child, I spent as much time as possible at Grandma and Grampa's farm. My parents and we children lived in a rented house in Mauston, about four miles from the farm. If I visited Grandma during the school year, Mom would pack a bag for me on Friday and I'd ride the school bus from St. Patrick's School in Mauston to the farm and return on Monday morning. I enjoyed riding the bus with the country kids.

Grandma, a medium-sized lady, carried herself with confidence. She had high cheek bones, deep set eyes, and full lips. She wore cotton house dresses, most floral in design protected by full-length aprons, cotton hose, and sturdy shoes. When I think back, I never saw her in anything but a dress and it didn't matter if she was cooking, gardening, or feeding the chickens. On rare occasions, I arose early enough to see her standing in front of the mirror doing her hair.

"Grandma, is it ok if I watch you?"

A nod of her head gave me permission.

As she brushed her long, thick, gray hair, she pulled it around over her shoulder to reach the ends. She stopped to remove hair from the brush and placed the hair in a porcelain hair receiver on her dresser. I watched her make one long braid, which she coiled at the crown of her head, holding the coil in place while securing it with hair combs. Wisps of hair framed her face. Grandma suffered a stroke at the age of sixty-five and asked Grampa to braid her hair. When he finished, she could see that he had braided her hair like he did the horses' tails—two strands.

I remember seeing her in a going-to-town or church dress, hose, low chunky heels, and always a hat held in place with glass-topped hatpins. Grandma's porcelain hatpin and ring holder now have a place in my hutch, always there to evoke a memory. There are twenty-one, four-inch hatpins: vibrant blues, purples, and greens; subtle whites and beige; a few with swirls like the planet,

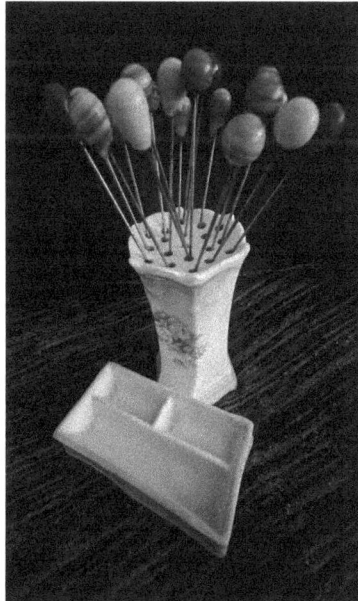

Saturn. When I'd watch her insert a hatpin of choice, it amazed me she did it without poking her scalp.

Every child should have a 'Grampa Debovik'— soft-spoken, gentle, and kind. Grampa was of medium height, balding, had a well-groomed moustache, and smiling eyes, his most striking feature. He worked hard, and treated his cows and horses with respect, giving his cows a well-deserved pat on the head or rear for giving an ample bucket of milk, or to the horse for pulling a wagon or corn-planter.

His daily garb consisted of bib overalls worn with a long-sleeved shirt, sleeves rolled up in hot weather. He dressed for the occasion when going to town or church, looking dapper in white shirt, tie, jacket and classic brimmed hat.

* * *

Memories are threads in the tapestry of life. Many of my fondest memories were woven together on my maternal grandparents' 120-acre property on County Road G, in the Lindina Township of Juneau County, about four miles southwest of Mauston, Wisconsin. The acreage was on both sides of the county road, and One Mile creek meandered through the southeast corner of the land.

A metal mailbox attached to a wooden pole, with the name DEBOVIK on it, stood firm across the road, letting you know you arrived. When Grandma sent me out to fetch the mail, she always told me to look both ways before crossing the road. Through the eyes of an eight-year-old, the dirt driveway from the house to the mailbox appeared to be a long travel adventure. Standing on tiptoes, I would reach for the tab and pull open the door. The prize might be a letter for Grandma and Grampa from their children in Chicago, a farm magazine, or *Women's Home Companion*.

Farm structures included a two-story house, a barn, machine shed, granary, corn crib, chicken house, and a pig pen. I remember a goose pinning me up against the machine shed and hissing at me when I made any movement. I froze in position and screamed for Grandma, who shooed him away. The goose became Sunday dinner.

My grandparents raised several Holstein cows, which are black and white, and Guernsey or Jersey, reddish-orange in color. They also had pigs, chickens, and two horses, Blackie and Queenie. The horses pulled the hay wagon, corn planter, plow, and the horse buggy.

The house, of medium-size, boasted an open porch on the south and west side, bordered by seasonal flowers, such as bleeding heart, hydrangea, and sedum. The porch served as the drying place for lace curtains stretched on frames, or fresh-picked mushrooms laid out on screens. Siblings, cousins, or neighbor girls and I played wedding on the porch using an old lace curtain for a veil, and whatever flower was in season for a bouquet. We would sing *Here comes the bride, fair, fat, and wide. Here comes the groom, skinny as a broom.*

A salesman's model of a cook stove

The first floor included a kitchen, pantry, dining room, parlor, two bedrooms, and a bathroom with a tub. Built-in cabinets divided the kitchen and dining room. The doors were wooden on the kitchen side and glass on the dining room side. The cabinet had a divider so when you were in the dining room, you saw the pretty China and glassware, and when in the kitchen, the everyday dishes. At one end was a flour bin.

Next to the cabinets, the wood stove and wood bin took center stage. Grandma had magical powers in knowing and obtaining the perfect temperature to produce golden dinner rolls, loaves of white and rye bread, braided coffee cakes, and pies. I had my very own small bread pan. The fragrance coming from the kitchen from bread baking in the oven told me it was time to get out the strawberry jam. I don't think the burners ever had time to cool down during canning season.

Grandma's children purchased an electric stove to make it 'easier' but it sat along the wall in the dining room, and was only used when cooking for the threshing crew or for lots of company.

Next to the stove was a single sink. A wooden footstool stood on the floor and a homemade apron hung on a hook ready and waiting for me when I helped with dishes. On the opposite wall, pantry

Example of a Hoosier cabinet (not my grandmother's actual one)

shelves extended almost to the ceiling; the remaining space was used for infrequently used items. I liked it when Grandma or Grampa lifted me up to reach something they needed.

Grandma's kitchen also contained a green metal, freestanding piece of furniture called a Hoosier cabinet. Floral mixing bowls sat on the top. Cupboards at the top and bottom were separated by a work space complete with a flour sifter.

I would often sit at this cabinet and eat my lunch. Canned cherries with the pits facilitated early math lessons. When I was served cherries for dessert, I would lay the discarded pits on the workspace counter. Grandma would say, "Rosie, put three pits in a row." And I would count out, "One, two, three."

"Now add two more." My little fingers picked up two more.

"How many are there now?"

"Five."

I still love cherries, and although I buy them without the pits, old memories come to mind.

During canning time, cheesecloth bags filled with cooked berries hung from the Hoosier cabinet drawer handles, the juice draining into a kettle to be made into jelly.

Across the room from the stove was the outside door and along the wall next to that, a small kitchen table.

On Sundays, I would sit in a chair placed near the stove so my mom or Grandma could heat the curling iron and give me a head full of curls. The alternative to the iron was curling with rags on Saturday evening. My hair would be dampened and the ends of a section of hair would be centered on the rag strip and wrapped around the strip until it reached the scalp. The ends of the strip were tied to secure it. Soon all my hair was in rag curls.

Another method was to place the ends of a section of hair at the center of the rag strip, wind one half of the rag around the hair up to the scalp, have me hold it in place while the other half of the rag was wrapped around, and then the ends were tied. Hair done up in rags was easy to sleep on and produced long-lasting curls like those worn by child star, Shirley Temple.

When Polish neighbors visited on Saturday nights, everyone congregated in the kitchen. Mr. Dudziak played his accordion and Mrs. Dudziak, their daughter, Mary, and Grandma and Grampa sang Polish songs. I enjoyed listening and watching Mr. Dudziak play the accordion, mesmerized by his finger and arm movements. I wondered what he was thinking when he closed his eyes and smiled. Remembering these times as part of my childhood, but writing as an adult, I think he savored creativity.

Evening visits ended with tea and a Polish dessert like poppyseed cake.

Walking into the dining room from the kitchen stood the rarely used electric stove to the left, China cabinet, open stairway, and bedroom to the right. A crystal chandelier hung above a wooden dining room table. About once a year, Grandma meticulously cleaned each crystal pendant, wearing white gloves.

A much-used Singer treadle sewing machine sat before the south-facing front window. I would pull up a chair when I saw Grandma remove the crocheted doily from the table-like top, lift the hinged lid and guide it to the left, reach in and pull the machine up, and set it in place. As she lubricated moving parts, the mild smell of oil filled the working area.

Before opening the machine, she laid out a pattern on fabric purchased in town or ordered from the Sears Roebuck catalog, pinned it in place, and cut out the pieces. Flour or seed bags with floral designs were recycled and transformed into dresses, aprons, or kitchen towels. I watched in awe as her adept fingers threaded the machine, placed the fabric under the pressor foot, reached up and pulled the pressor foot lever down, pulled the hand wheel toward her with her right hand, put pressure on the treadle with her right foot, reaching desired sewing speed. *Magic.*

She sewed dresses and full-length aprons for herself and dresses for my sister, Mary, and me. I loved when I heard, "OK, Rosie, come by me." Grandma would hold the dress against my body front and back, turning her head this way and that way, and then, "*Bardzo dobry.* Take the dress, put it on and I'll mark the hem." *Bardzo dobry* is Polish for very good.

21

Children's dresses usually had a white collar, and ties at the waist pulled to the back and tied in a bow. I adored my beautiful, white, First Holy Communion dress. I wore the dress on that special day in 1944, and whenever I could, I convinced Mom or Grandma. "Please, please can I wear my beautiful dress to church?"

Scraps of material left over from sewing projects were transformed into braided rugs. I enjoyed getting down on the floor by one of the rugs and squeal with delight as I identified fabric from one of my or Grandma's handmade dresses. A braided rug provided a soft place alongside my bed to kneel on when I said night prayers.

A wooden crank wall phone had its place on the wall to the right of the sewing machine. A 1940s wall phone, made of wood, with approximate dimensions of 18 x 8 x 4, had a hand-held receiver on the left side, a hand crank on the right, and mouthpiece and ringers on the front as well as a slanted shelf. Being on a party line—a

Example of a wall phone

party meaning three or four others—required the courtesy of lifting the receiver before making a call to assure access, and not listening to party-line conversations. I'm not 100% positive but I think three long hand cranks and two short hand cranks connected you to the Debovik residence.

A potbelly stove, along the side of the stairway, was always ready to be stoked up to warm little bodies in the morning, warm cold hands after playing in the snow, or to heat a pot of tea.

Beautiful teacup and saucer

Matching plate

I drank my first cup of tea at about the age of six. I remember best the metal tea holder filled with tea leaves and the metal chain dangling over the edge of the teapot. When brewed, Grandma poured tea into pretty China cups, added milk and sugar, and we sipped and enjoyed. I proudly display those cups, saucers, small plates, teapot, and sugar and creamer in my hutch. The design is hand-painted white flowers and a colorful bird on a light blue background, and an orange trim.

Area rugs covered the floors of the living room. I enjoyed pushing the Bissell carpet cleaner with its harsh sound as I moved it back and forth. Summer cleaning of rugs, draped over a clothesline and smacked with a long-handled rug

Player piano

beater, ended up being fun if a cousin or sibling joined in.

A player piano filled one corner of the room, graced by a fern atop a pedestal. Player pianos are magical. A paper roller filled with intricately spaced holes was inserted in its proper place, a foot pedal pushed, and ghostly fingers moved up and down to play *Beautiful Dreamer* or *K-K-K-Katy*, or other popular music selections. My sister, Mary, three years younger than I, loved the song, *Ramona*, and being too little to reach the pedals with her feet, kneeled on the floor and used her hands. After Grandma positioned the roller, I seated myself at the edge of the piano bench, stretched my leg out to press the pedal, and just pretended to be a pianist.

A crocheted throw draped over the back of an overstuffed chair, built-in bookshelves, and a beaded floor lamp invited occupancy. I loved curling up in the chair, leaning across the armrest, scanning the books, choosing one, most above my reading level, but trying to sound out words. An illustrated children's book, *The Timbertoes* by Aldredge, McKee, and Gee, describing the adven-tures of a wooden family, Mr. and Mrs. Timbertoe and their children and dog, delighted me.

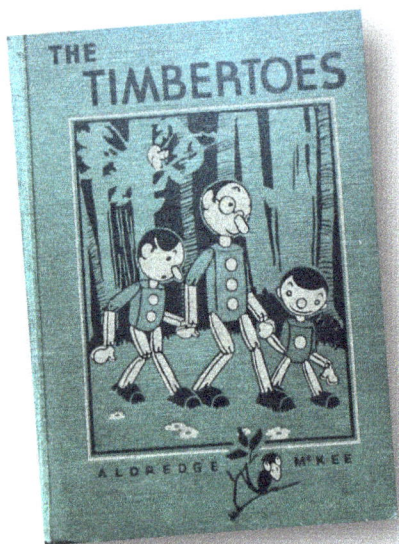

The book is out of print, but I found one on eBay at a reasonable price in April of 2023.

The chair served another purpose—a hiding place. Living on a farm in the area, Aunt Isabel, Uncle Art, and cousins Margie, Tony, and Eddie often visited. Toward the end of the evening, Margie and I snuggled ourselves up in the chair, hiding under the throw, both hoping she could spend the night, and then, "Marge, time to go." We giggled, burrowed down, waited to be uncovered because sometimes the grown-ups surprised us and said yes.

I remember a souvenir gifted to Grandma from Florida; a fuzzy little monkey, made from pipe cleaners, with arms wrapped around the trunk of a palm tree. Plump, arching, green pipe cleaners formed the palms. It's a memory my sister Mary and I hold in our hearts.

Grandma and Grampa's bedroom, off the living room, spoke simplicity—a bed with a feather tick cover, a dresser top displaying a matching brush, comb, and mirror; a floral porcelain hair receiver, and a hatpin holder. A Blessed Mother picture hung on the wall. A sewing basket in the closet held embroidery floss, crochet cotton, yarn, pretty buttons—all the fixings for creative projects. Grandma saved empty wooden thread spools and Grampa attached four nails to the top to make a spool knitter. With a spool knitter, I'd knit a long coil and make little rugs for my cardboard doll house.

An open stairway led to the second floor. To the right of the landing at the top of the stairs was a small bedroom and to the left, a bedroom that extended almost across the length of the house. At the east end of the bedroom, a door led to a storage room. After Grandma died in September 1947, Mom and her sister Isabel sat on the floor divvying up Christmas ornaments. Laughter replaced sad looks on their faces as they tried to divide cellophane tinsel. The more they pulled, the more entangled it became. Standing at the doorway, we kids chuckled when Aunt Isabel pushed the tinsel toward her sister, "Eleanor, take it all."

Two places fascinated me in Grandma and Grampa's house—the North Room and the cellar.

The North Room, located on the second level, provided a space to store or cure homemade kielbasa, bloodwurst, and white sausage. Homemade sausage casings were made from the intestines of butchered cows and pigs. The cast-iron sausage stuffer was curved with a large opening at the top to put in the sausage and a smaller opening at the end to attach the intestine. A pump-looking handle with a circular disk forced the sausage into the intestine. When the sausage reached the desired length, Grandma secured it with sturdy string. I would wait patiently for her to say, "Rosie, get a chair to kneel on and help me put sausage in the grinder."

The cellar had two rooms. In the fall, before you ever got to the bottom of the steps to the cellar, the smell of stored apples picked from the orchard welcomed you. A milk separator sat along the wall. I grew up drinking raw milk, meaning not pasteurized. A device called the milk separator, separated milk into cream and skim milk. Some of the skimmed milk was consumed while the rest utilized to feed calves and pigs. The cream was saved to make butter or to put on strawberries in the summer. Grandma made her own butter and sometimes she would let me push up and down on the butter churn, probably for a few seconds so as to keep the process going, but to me, I made butter.

In the second room, shelves along two walls were filled with hundreds of fruit jars, colors of the contents like an artist's palette. Then came the potato and carrot bins. Carrots were buried in sand. My favorite memory in the cellar was watching Grandma put shredded cabbage in a stoneware crock, setting a weight on top, and then checking the fermentation process on a regular basis. We were rewarded with pork hocks and homemade sauerkraut. Yum!

Songs and Prayers

Grandma and Grampa's house spoke of their Catholic faith. A picture of the *Blessed Mother* hung in their room and a crucifix, *Christ Knocking on the Door* in a second bedroom, and *Guardian Angel Crossing Bridge with Children* in a third bedroom. At bedtime, besides saying the *Now I Lay Me Down To Sleep* prayer, Grandma would sing me this song:

Stars are the windows of heaven
Where Angels peek through
Up in the sky they keep an eye
On kids like me and you

They cry each time we are naughty
Their tear drops are the rain
But when we're good
They are smiling and they shine again

Stars are the windows of heaven
Where Angels peek through

I loved the idea of angels watching over me, especially if I was sleeping alone in a bedroom.

Another song I enjoyed was *When the Red, Red, Robin Comes Bob, Bob, Bobbing Along* by Irving Berlin, often sung by my mom when she woke me up. The lyrics I loved the most were: *Wake up, wake up you sleepyhead. Get up, get up, get out of bed.*

Love of Nature and Gardening

I owe my love of nature and gardening to Mom, Dad, and Grandma Debovik. Winter never seemed long if we kids had something to anticipate, such as a sweet potato vine. Mom cut off the end of a sweet potato, inserted four toothpicks around the middle of the potato to prop it on the rim of a vase, and placed enough water in the vase so the bottom of the potato could sit on the water. We learned patience as we waited about a month to see roots and vine sprouts emerge. Once that happened, vines grew in abundance.

Dad's gardens were a sight to behold. He planted zinnias at the ends of the rows of vegetables. A weed would not dare enter.

One of the first flowers I learned about was trailing arbutus. Mary Dyer, Credentialed Garden Writer, says according to plant folklore, the arbutus or mayflower plant was the first spring-blooming plant the Pilgrims saw after their first arduous winter in the new country. It appears in early spring and its home is the forest floor.

Mom or Grandma, or the two of them together, and I would trek to the woods bordering the farm fields. I would be wearing my farmer overalls, a warm jacket, and rubber, over-the-shoe, buckle boots. Our journey took me down the driveway, across the road, and what seemed a long, long ways along the field until we reached the woods.

"Rosie, watch where you step. It's a little plant."

Leaves leftover from fall crunched beneath my boots. I watched ahead so I wouldn't trip over a dead branch or log. Patches of snow remained.

Grandma stopped, bent down and with excitement in her voice, "I found one. Come and look. Rosie, we can't pick it so lie on your tummy and smell it."

I stretched out and inched closer until my nose almost became part of the flower. The best smell ever. I didn't want to move. Even today, I can close my eyes and remember the sweet scent of the delicate white blooms.

In my adult life, I had the word *Arbutus* on my license plate.

Today, I am an *avid* gardener, which means I love everything there is to love about gardening: catalogs, garden centers, planting, watching, fertilizing, transplanting, and yes, weeding, and always finding room for one more plant. Thank you, Grandma, for taking me by the hand, stopping to introduce me to the plants, telling me their names: bleeding heart, hydrangea, buttercup, lilac, and the list goes on. There was a plant my sibs and I called 'frog tongue'—its real name, *sedum*. We'd break off a leaf, and gently squeeze it between our thumb and pointer finger until the leaf felt squishy without breaking the membrane. We'd put the end up to our lips and gently blow. The leaf expanded and looked like a frog tongue.

Grandma and Grampa had huge gardens that required hours of care. Everyone of us had a job. We little kids could pick potato bugs from the plants and place them in a fruit jar for disposal.

Melons were grown and sold to local grocers and Grandma was the business lady. I remember sitting at the dining room table listening to her talk to a businessman as they negotiated terms of sale. Being little, I didn't understand all they were talking about, but I knew when she disagreed.

"*Nie,*" she said with a confident voice in Polish.

I knew she meant business because Grandma and Grampa spoke English well, but if we were doing something we shouldn't be, we heard '*nie*' as well. Somehow it had more impact than the English '*no*'.

A stand of shagbark hickory trees grew on the farm land and picking hickory nuts in the fall was another adventure with Grandma. We put on our straw hats, carried drinking water in a fruit jar, each had a pail—mine smaller, and off we went.

Picking hickory nuts required bending and kneeling to gather them off the ground.

"Rosie, pick up the nuts that are green, have no spots, and aren't broken. If you see light-colored nuts, pick them up too; the husk has already fallen off. Don't pick up nuts with holes; they probably have bugs inside." In my memory, it was a perfect day, hearing the plunk of a nut hitting the bottom of the bucket and the changing sound as the bucket became fuller, a cow mooing in the distance, Mrs. Kasper, from a neighboring farm, seeing us and shouting, "Yoo-hoo," and waving, and the best part being with a grandma I loved.

After the nuts were taken to the house, Grandma removed the outer shells so the harvested nuts could be laid out to dry for a couple of weeks. And then one evening after supper, Grandma would say, "We're going to crack hickory nuts tonight."

First, a protective cover was placed on the dining room table before we set out the supplies: anvil or brick, nut picker, bowl for the shells, and a fruit jar to hold the nutmeats. I loved sitting there, feeling the warmth of the potbelly stove, ready to help.

Hickory nut shells are tough and require a just-right tap of a hammer to hit the flat side of the nut placed on an anvil or brick. Grandma cracked several nuts and then we would use a pointed metal nut-picker tool to remove the nutmeat from the shell. I'd squeal with delight if they came out whole, which didn't happen often. Because we had collected so many nuts, this task was repeated several evenings. Stored hickory nuts were used in cookies, cakes, and for a snack.

Research tells us hickory nuts are a highly nutritious and tasty food. They contain as much protein as chicken and are a great source of minerals, especially calcium, magnesium, phosphorous, and potassium. They are a good source of folate, one of the vitamins important to expectant mothers.

* * *

Wild forest mushrooms are essential ingredients of the Polish culinary tradition. To some Poles, the word mushroom literally means *"may the forest provide."* They are pickled, used in soups, stews, pierogi (filled dumplings), scrambled eggs, mixed with sauerkraut, and the list goes on.

Mushroom hunting was usually a group activity with family and friends. I was too little to collect mushrooms, as edible mushroom identification was critical. Grandma cleaned the picked mushrooms with a damp cloth and then spread them out to dry on framed screens placed on two sawhorses on the front porch.

* * *

Apple, cherry, and plum trees grew in an orchard next to the farmhouse. The orchard provided a great place to hide when playing hide-and-seek. My friend, Barbara Kasper, and I could pretend we were Hansel and Gretel lost in the "forest." If it was fall, we could eat windfall apples. Under one of the cherry trees, Laddie, a collie, was buried. A small garden pond bordered the orchard where one might see a goldfish peeking around a lily pad.

Along the full length of the garden were Concord grape vines. One day, my sibs and I came into the house and were shocked when Grandma said, "You were eating the grapes." How did she know? We had sat on the side where we weren't in view from the house window. Could it be that our lips and tongues were blue?

The Wonders of the Milky Way

I am swallowed up by a feather-tick comforter, which is wonderful in an unheated bedroom, until you have to slide out from under it an inch at a time, dreading your feet touching the cold floor.

Mom is calling. "Rosie, wake up. I have something special to show you."

Opening my eyes, I say, "It's still dark."

"Hurry, I'll help you get your socks and shoes on. We're going outside."

"In my nightgown?"

Mom knelt by the bedside. My feet stuck out from the covers; the rest of me did not want to get out. She slipped on my socks and shoes.

"Let's go."

We went downstairs into the kitchen. Mom grabbed my coat, holding it open ready for my arms to slip into the sleeves. She placed a cap on my head, giving an extra tug over my ears, put on her coat, and out the back door we went. A kerosene lamp sat on the ground and illuminated Grandma and Grampa, who were huddled together looking up at the sky.

Mom bent down, her head close to mine, and pointed upwards. It was like magic—a hazy highway across the sky. I learned later in life that this "highway" is a galaxy made up of several billion stars, including the sun.

I don't know if it was late evening or early morn, or how the grown-ups knew the Milky Way would be visible, but it didn't matter. What mattered was they gave a small child a rare glimpse of our amazing universe.

City Kin Come to the Farm

The chickens clucked, the cows mooed, the horses whinnied, sensing it was not an ordinary day. Vehicles, some with Illinois license plates, lined the driveway. Hugs, Polish dialect, squealing cousins; all announcing the weekend the Chicago relatives came to the farm. The family included uncles and aunts, and— cousins:

- Frank and Julia Czajka—Edward and Vivian
- John and Celia Czajka—Donald and Arlene
- Earl and Clara Schabert—Earl and Loraine
- Arthur and Regina Lamberti—Arthur and Theresa
- Anthony and Doris Czajka—Phillip, Virginia, and James
- Felix and Martha Wisniewski—Delores and Richard
- Arthur and Isabel Hess—Marguerite, Anthony, and Edward
- Frederick and Eleanor Steinmetz—Rose, Mary, Fred, Susan, Barbara (Rita and Patricia were born after Grandma died.)

Not everyone came every year but the average was probably twenty-five. Cousins ranged in age from infant to seventeen years.

To save wear and tear of guests, especially children, from trampling through the house to wash hands or get a drink, an enamel basin of water, bar soap, and a towel sat on a small wooden table near the back door of the house, and a drinking ladle hung on the spout of the nearby water pump.

After food donations were carried into the house, and bathroom stops taken, the aunts gathered in the kitchen or on the front porch and seemed to talk all at once, and in Polish, hands moving as fast as the spoken word.

The uncles headed to the horseshoe pit, which was set up at the edge of the county road between the driveway and the field. *Horseshoes* is a lawn game played with actual horseshoes between two people or two teams of two people. The players take turns throwing the horseshoes at stakes placed forty feet apart, ideally to make a ringer or get closest to the stake. Points are earned. It wasn't long before the clink and clank of horseshoes could be heard. When a ringer was made, there was hooting and hollering, pats on the back, as well as groans from the opposing team.

We kids had to make our own fun. Grampa had a two-wheeled cart with a seat and long wooden shafts that could be attached to and pulled by a horse. Our cousin Donny, age nine, decided he or another *older* cousin could be the horse. That year, the reunion must have been in late August because acorns had started to fall.

Donny instructed us to find as many acorns as possible; he placed them in a container. There were single acorns as well as doubles and triples. We formed a line, and when it was our turn, we reached into the bucket, not looking, and pulled out an acorn or acorns. One acorn—one loop around the barnyard, two acorns—two loops, and three acorns—three loops. One by one, we took our turns, crawled up into the seat, Donny centered himself between the shafts, took hold, and around we went, laughing and squealing.

At one of the reunions, the older cousins headed into the barn and of course, I followed. They started up the ladder to go up into the hay loft. When they got there, they looked through the opening," Come on, Rose. You can make it." I was seven at the time and had been told by Grandma and Grampa not to go up there unless they or Mom were with me.

"No, I'm not supposed to. I'll stay down here and eat my orange," I said as I started peeling it.

"It's okay. We're older and we can help you." Older was any age between nine and twelve. The *real older* cousins were playing horseshoes with their dads and uncles.

I made it to about the third rung and slipped, falling to the barn floor. I started to cry, "My arm hurts. I want to go by my mom."

"You can't tell anyone you were on the ladder," said Donny.

"But I was."

"Say you slipped on your orange peel."

Donny and the others helped me to my feet and walked me up to the house. I walked into the kitchen, cradling my arm. Mom, Grandma, and aunts all asked at once, "What happened?" and cousins in unison said, "We were in the barn and she slipped on her orange peel."

Mom and I got into someone's vehicle and drove to Dr. Griffin's office, a small, white house on State Street in Mauston. That day, I learned about greenstick fractures and splints. Years later, when I was a teen, Mom and I were talking about that day. "I saw right through that story," she said with a grin on her face.

I believe at every reunion there was a baseball game; the expanse of yard between the house and road became the baseball field. Adults and children alike played. One time when I was up to bat, I must have hit a bee instead of the ball and was stung on my arm. Mom applied a baking soda paste on the sting and I went back out and played.

I don't recall if we ate outside or inside but the food choices probably included baked chicken, beef and horseradish sauce, sausages snuggled in sauerkraut, potato salad, cucumber salad, deviled eggs, pierogi, a variety of pickles, including watermelon rind pickles, homemade white and the best rye bread ever, and plump apple pies with a golden crust.

I was under the age of ten at these reunions so I don't know where everyone stayed for the weekend. I'm assuming some of the relatives stayed at Aunt Isabel or Aunt Doris' home since they lived nearby. Some of the cousins stayed over and I remember we kneeled at the head of the stairs, and peeked through the rails to watch the grown-ups play a card game called pinochle. It wasn't long before we were spotted.

"Get back to bed!"

Going to the Juneau County Fair

Grandma and Grampa Debovik pulled up in front of our house with the horse and buggy. As I ran out the door, Grampa, wearing dark trousers, a long-sleeved white shirt, and black dress hat, got out of the buggy and laid the reins on the ground. Queenie, the horse, would stay put until we were ready to leave for the fairgrounds. He then went to the other side, extended his arm for Grandma to hang on to as she stepped down. She wore a flowered dress, sturdy shoes, and a wide-brimmed straw hat.

Grandma or Grampa Debovik, or both, would come into town and pick up my sister Mary and me; we were the two oldest in our family, at eight and five. Four-year-old Freddy might have gone too, but I don't remember. Susan would've been a baby in 1944. Before leaving for the fairgrounds, Grandma reminded us to bring our sun umbrellas. Of note, whenever Grandma or Grampa came to town to visit us, Grampa always brought a small bag of circus peanut candy or chocolate vanilla creams.

When I was a child in the 1940s, attending the Juneau County Fair was the highlight of the summer. For most country and townsfolk, the fair

47

was the only summer holiday. The first Juneau County Cattle Show and Fair took place October 3 and 4, 1866, and has continued at its original location at the south end of Mauston.

As we entered the fairgrounds, I looked up, and the towering Ferris wheel filled me with excitement.

A burly operator of the Strongman game was shouting, "Step right up! Test your strength." Confident-looking men, with shirt sleeves rolled up, stood in line, waiting to show-off.

I looked this way and that way, hardly able to take it all in. Suddenly, Grandma took my hand and whisked me past a row of attractions, but I remember seeing billboards for the *Fat Lady* and *Sword Swallower*.

We first visited the stock pavilion. Smells of fresh hay, animal excrement, and sweat filled the air. I'm sure as a young child I uttered, "P U." We watched young and older adults grooming calves, cows, pigs, and horses, all hoping for a blue-ribbon. Horses' manes were braided and their coats brushed to a fine sheen. The pavilion reverberated with oinks, moos, and whinnies.

Grampa went on to the cattle auction while Grandma and I sauntered through the Home-making pavilion, lined with rows of tables displaying artfully designed afghans, crocheted doilies, and intricately embroidered pillow cases, as well as pies and preserves in a rainbow of colors.

The rides are what I looked forward to the most. The rides I remember were the Ferris wheel, the Tilt-A-Whirl, and the merry-go-round. The best was saved until last—the pony rides and cotton candy.

Holding my ticket tightly, I stood in line waiting for the Ferris wheel to stop and riders get off. One by one, new passengers got on. The Ferris wheel slowly rotated so the next seat was positioned over the platform. Grandma and I walked and stood with our backs to the seat, sat down and the operator secured the safety bar. Grandma would tell me, "No rocking the seat." I probably had my fingers wrapped around the safety bar and was afraid to take a breath for fear of moving. I loved when we stopped at the top and could view the city of Mauston, St. Patrick's church steeple, corn and wheat fields, families scurrying below, and horse and buggies and cars parked at the fairground. Calliope music from the merry-go-round set the mood.

The Tilt-a-Whirl was a raised wavy platform with about seven free-spinning cars. To get in a car, you had to walk up some stairs and onto a narrow walkway around the outer edge of the platform. The floor of the platform rotated and each seat also went around. You shifted your weight to change directions or go faster. I know Grandma loved the ride as much as I did as she laughed and squealed. She usually was a bit more stoic.

The next ride was the merry-go-round. The merry-go-round attracted all ages with a selection of beautiful carousel horses, bench seats, and the steam organ music of the calliope. When the merry-go-round stopped, riders got off and new passengers, especially children, scurried along the platform trying to decide which horse they wanted to sit on. I remember having only a few minutes to decide but they were all so beautiful: white, brown, black, spotted, jeweled, and each saying, "Choose me."

Once I selected the one I wanted, Grandma would assist me in getting on and when the merry-go-round rotated, I hung on tightly to the pole. Grandma stood by me resting her arm on the back of the horse. The magic began. Up and down, round and round, traveling where my imagination led me, taking time to wave at Grampa as we passed. The merry-go-round slowed. I knew this ride was a memory until next year's fair.

The pony rides delighted me the most. There were real ponies. Six to eight ponies waited for riders in a circular fenced in area. An attendant walked me to a pony, soothed anxieties, and lifted me onto the saddle. I loved the smell of the leather saddle, the feel of the rhythmic pace, my little fingers grasping the pommel, and smiling at Grandma and Grampa as I passed. The attendant stood in the center, keeping a watchful eye on us children and the ponies. My sister, Mary, shared her memory of the squeak of the leather saddle as the pony went round and round.

Grandstand shows allowed fairgoers time to sit and rest while being entertained. In 2015, a booklet was put together for the 150th celebration of the Juneau County Fair, complete with photos and a decade-by-decade narrative. In the 1940s, when I attended the fair with my grandparents or parents, the entertainment may have been a horse pulling contest, baseball game, boxing meet, harness racing, a Tug-of-War fest, or local entertainment. My memory is telling me I saw an awesome performance by a baton twirler. (I received clarification from Rose Clark, Archivist, Juneau County Historical Museum in Mauston, Wisconsin.)

Last, but not least, was eating cotton candy—fluffy, pink, sticky—and best of all the feeling when you pinched off strands of it, popped it in your mouth, and poof—just like that— it melted.

Threshing Day

Neighboring farmers and their wives arrived early to Grandma and Grampa's farm, some in cars, some with horse and buggy. Several of the women brought their children. Area farmers assisted each other in the harvesting of the wheat.

The farmer who owned the thresher towed it into the field by tractor. The women, already wearing their aprons, went into the house to help Grandma start preparing the food for lunch. Some carried pies with golden crusts, plump with apple, cherry, or mincemeat filling. As a child watching this, I could only hope there would be pie left by the time it was my turn to eat. I didn't watch for long as all of us children were ushered outside to play and not be underfoot.

When the men came in from the field, they washed their hands in a basin set out by the back door. They also brushed the chaff from their clothes.

The dining room table was a delight to behold. There were steaming bowls of mashed potatoes, squash, and gravy. Platters held roast pork. A bowl of purple cabbage gave color to the table. Applesauce made from the apples in Grandma and Grampa's orchard waited to be ladled onto someone's plate. An assortment of pickles filled a relish dish: watermelon pickles, sweet, and dill pickles. There were breads and dinner rolls, all homemade. A tempting assortment of pies and desserts filled the top of the sideboard.

The men seated themselves at the table and said *Grace*. The best waitresses they probably would ever have—the womenfolk—served them. I don't know how the men had the energy to return to the field after all they ate. The women ate next, and while they started doing the dishes, we children ate. There was always enough food.

At the end of the day, much gratitude was expressed, and plans were made for the next threshing assignment.

Threshing machine

1915 photo of threshing day. Photo courtesy of the Farmington
Historical Society, Washington Co. Wisconsin)

Going to the Feed Mill

Clip clop, clip clop, clip clop
The rhythm of hooves upon the road.
Queenie happy for a day away from the farm,
as was my grandma.

Her favorite go-to-town hat
held in place with a hatpin.
The blue striped round glass
glistening in the sun.

Reins held comfortably in her weathered hands
able to adjust speed, stops, and turns
with subtle movements of her wrists.
Years of practice.

I, sitting tall beside her
wearing bibbed overalls
and a flour-sack-fabric blouse,
feeling special.

Soon we will be at the feed mill
the earthy smell of grain forever
etched in my memory.
A hefty man placing a bag of chicken feed
on the floor of the buggy.

And the best part of the day
going to the drugstore
for a chocolate ice cream cone.
A ten-cent treasure.

Entertaining Ourselves on the Farm

What did children do to busy themselves in the 1940s when televisions and cellphones didn't exist? The farm became the playground and farm kids found ways to challenge equilibrium, coordination, and creativity.

On my grandparents' farm, a tire swing hung from a sturdy limb of an oak tree on the south side of the driveway. I loved positioning myself on top of the tire, legs dangling, and hands gripping the thick sisal rope, and having a parent, grandparent, sibling, or neighbor friend twist the tire around several rotations, and then, lifting my feet and spinning wildly when they let go. The swing could be relaxing just sitting inside the opening, arms wrapped around the tire, gently steering by pushing my feet along the ground. If it had recently rained, the tire needed to be tipped to drain the water; if I forgot, the first motion of the swing resulted in a wet bottom.

* * *

Walking through the cow pastures where bumps formed as a result of cows taking the same route to and from the barn, challenged coordination. When cousins gathered together on the farm, it became a game to walk bump to bump without slipping in the groove between the bumps. Of course, we were barefoot and most likely stepped in a cowpie or two; maybe that's the reason for my size-9 shoes.

* * *

One didn't need playground equipment if you had trees. My sister Mary and I loved climbing trees. A favorite tall pine tree bordered the pigpen and we climbed a nearby fence to reach the lowest limb and scaled like monkeys upward. Watching the pigs below us snorting and rolling in the mud entertained us. It wasn't Grandma's favorite tree for us to climb for fear we would fall into the pigpen.

* * *

I think we had more snow in the 40s. My neighbor friend, Barbara, lived on the farm uphill from my grandparents. When I'd come to the farm on a weekend after a significant snowfall, Barbara and I got on our sleds on their land, and steered our way to the bottom, *even over a barbwire fence—yes, the snow was that deep.*

* * *

Another neighbor family, the Bennetts, owned a horse-drawn sleigh. Maybe it was called a horse-drawn wagon but it had sled runners on it and seats inside. I only rode in it once but I never forgot the experience. Mr. and Mrs. Bennett and their sons, Robin and Andy, and Grampa Bennett came to the farm to pick up Grandma, Grampa and me. Greetings were exchanged. The two horses stood patiently, visible steamy breaths coming from their nostrils, as I was hoisted into the sleigh, and Grandma and Grampa climbed in.

Mr. Bennett and his father sat in the front seat, Grampa, Grandma, and Mrs. Bennett in the middle seat, and we three youngsters in the back. We covered ourselves with scratchy wool blankets. Grandma probably needed the blanket the most, as she wore a dress, unlike me with coat, snow pants, knitted hat and mittens, a scarf wrapped around my face—and rubber buckle boots over my shoes. Metal handrails attached to the seats gave us something to hang onto as Mr. Bennett picked up the reins, gave them a gentle shake, and the sleigh lurched forward.

Reaching the end of the driveway, the horses turned left onto county Road G. No one spoke those first few minutes; young and old alike entranced by the snow crunching under the runners, the muffled rhythmical hoof sounds, and darkness except for the light of the moon and a hanging lantern.

Mr. Bennett turns his head and says, "We will ride to our house and the Mrs. will serve hot apple cider and gingerbread cake and then I'll take you back."

The horses seemed to know when we reached the driveway as the pace of their gait increased. Mr. Bennett pulled the reins back, the horses slowed and stopped in front of the house. He stepped out of the sleigh, tethered the horses to a hitching post, and offered a hand as we took turns getting out. Of course, Robin and Andy, jumped out first.

"Thanks, Mr. Bennett."

"You're welcome."

After we entered the house and removed boots, hats, and mittens, it wasn't long before Mrs. Bennett put the cider on the stove to heat, and set out dessert plates on the long wooden table in the kitchen. "Go to the parlor. Grampa Bennett will play his violin."

Grandma Debovik stayed in the kitchen to help out, and the rest of us gathered in the parlor. We kids made ourselves comfortable on a circular braided rug and Mr. Bennett and Grampa Debovik sat on a sofa.

"How about I play *Jingle Bells?*"

As he played, we sang along. Occasionally, he'd put the violin down, lean over the edge of his rocker, and spit into a shiny pot on the floor. I thought he might be sick. He must have seen the look on my face as he laughed and said, "Don't worry. That's tobacco juice." Later in life, I learned the shiny pot had a name—spittoon.

"Come everyone. Dessert is ready."

The hot cider and gingerbread warmed my tummy before going back out into the winter air. Mrs. Bennett and Grampa Bennett stayed behind. The rest of us returned to the sleigh for the trip home. I heard Grandma and Grampa say *'Dziekuje'*, Polish for thank you.

I suppose the grown-ups chatted and we kids giggled as we continued on our magical ride.

We returned to the farm, and thoughts of cuddling up under the feather tick quilt and reliving the sleigh ride filled my mind.

* * *

Popular games provided entertainment, namely Dominos, Chinese Checkers, Pick-up Sticks, jigsaw puzzles, and cards. My favorite card games were Old Maid, War, Solitaire, and 500 Rummy. Another pastime was folding a 4 x 4-inch piece of paper twice and then cutting off a corner and combinations of cut out triangles, half-circles, or straight cuts along the edges—when unfolded, they made a snowflake. Pages from outdated wallpaper sample books made the most beautiful snowflakes.

Paper dolls were also popular. They could be purchased, but my friend Barbara and I had just as much fun with paper dolls created by her mother. Mrs. Kasper put her artistic talents to work as she sketched figures on cardboard, cut them out, and drew hair and faces. She cut out coats, dresses, hats, skirts, trousers, and shoes from Sears and Montgomery Ward catalogs. As she cut out pictures of clothing, she purposely made rectangular tabs to attach to the paper dolls. We could spend hours sitting on the braided circular rug in the parlor, dressing our pretend families.

* * *

I remember an unexpected adventure when I heard Grandma say, "Rose, I haven't seen the barn cat for a few days. Maybe she had her kittens."

"Where would they be?"

"Probably in the hayloft."

I laughed. "Can cats climb a ladder?"

"Oh, yes. Very well."

We went into the barn and to the ladder; I climbed first with Grandma right behind me. I loved the smell of the hay, something warm and fuzzy about it.

"Look carefully. If she had her babies, she will be curled up in some hay, probably in a corner."

Grandma was right. In the far corner, Momma cat could be seen stretched out on her side with a pile of kittens close to her.

"Grandma, they're so little. One-two-three-four! They would fit in my hand. Can I pick one up?"

"No, no. Not yet. In a couple weeks."

"How come their eyes are closed?"

"Kitties are born with their eyes closed and ears folded, which means they are blind and deaf for a week or two. Momma cat will take good care of them. We'd better go now."

I wouldn't trade the many experiences I had on the farm. It truly provided the groundwork for my love of nature and animals.

Stereoscope of Christmas Memories

Did our family celebrate Christmas both at our house and our grandparents' home during the ten years of my life while Grandma was alive? Memories come to mind in both settings.

December 1940, at the age of three and a half, is my earliest memory of Christmas. We lived in a small house on Tremont Street in Mauston, Wisconsin. Mom and Dad were sitting on a couch, Mom holding my eight-month-old sister, Mary.

"Santa didn't bring me a sled," I said in a sad voice.

Dad answered, "I think I heard sleigh bells. Let's look outside."

Dad and I walked out the front door, I in my pajamas and slippers. Mom, holding Mary wrapped in a blanket, stood in the doorway.

"A sled, a sled!" As I walked towards the sled, I saw a shiny bell lying in the snow.

"Daddy, look!" I held the bell in my tiny, cold hand.

"Santa must have lost one of his sleigh bells. Show Mommy. I'll put the sled on the porch." Dad explained. "You can try it out in the morning."

My parents created a special Christmas. I no longer have the bell but I treasured it for years.

Weeks before Christmas, Mom, Grandma, and Aunt Isabel gathered to make fruitcake. I wish I had better recall of the process. I do know some of the ingredients were candied fruit, nuts, raisins, cake batter, sugar, and alcohol such as brandy or whiskey for preserving the cake. The cake was wrapped and stored in a cool, dark place for a couple of months and occasionally had to be unwrapped and brushed with alcohol, which helped the aging process, helped preserve it and kept it from getting moldy. Fruitcake is one of those desserts you love or hate—I liked it.

I associate mincemeat pie with Christmas. Grandma canned her own mincemeat made from beef, suet, fruit, spices, raisins, and alcohol. The combination of these ingredients gave the mixture its hard-to-describe, distinctive flavor.

A bowl filled with walnuts, Brazil nuts, pecans, filberts, and peanuts in the shell had its place on the dining room table, along with a nutcracker, nut picks, and a bowl for the shells. I loved the challenge of cracking the walnuts and pecans without breaking the nutmeat. Not easy!

Christmas hard candy, colorful with flower imprints, ribbon shapes, and soft fruity fillings satisfied our sweet tooth. Mom and Grandma made seafoam, also known as angel or fairy food, a popular homemade candy.

During the Christmas season, a small Santa house large enough for Santa and a child, stood on the grounds of the Juneau County Courthouse in Mauston. Children, dressed in warm clothing, stood in line and waited with anticipation to talk with Santa. Later, in a large courthouse room, children received goodie bags from Santa.

I surmise we went out to Grandma and Grampa's farm on the day of Christmas Eve, and returned home after midnight Mass at St. Patrick's Church to celebrate Christmas Day.

Christmas Eve was filled with much symbolism, and the most important holiday for Christians of Polish descent. The Polish name for the traditional Christmas Eve supper is *Wigilia*. Dinner consisted of twelve meatless entrees, which represented the twelve apostles. I remember mushroom soup, beet soup with dumplings, cabbage, herring, baked fish, pierogi, and poppyseed cake. A small amount of hay, placed under the tablecloth, represented Jesus' birth in a stable. There was also a space, complete with China and silverware, reserved for an unexpected guest or stranger.

Before the meal started, a thin baked wafer without much taste, called *oplatek*, was shared with everyone other as turns were taken breaking off a piece of the wafer, eating it, and extending wishes for the upcoming year.

After the meal, the family gathered in the living room. The tree stood in the corner of the living room adorned with ornaments, cellophane tinsel, and clip-on candles. My favorite ornament was a blown-glass bird with a shimmering spun glass tail. A round mirror with ice-skating figures had a special spot under the tree and a special place in my heart. I don't have my grandma's rink, but skaters and a rink are a part of my Christmas village.

Grandma would say, "Children, find a spot to sit on the rug. It's time to light the candles on the tree."

"Won't the tree burn?" someone usually asked.

"No, not if you're really quiet and don't move around."

She'd carefully light the candles, say something in Polish, and after a few seconds, used a candle snuffer to gently put out the flame. I don't believe I ever blinked. I didn't want to miss the magic.

Gifts were opened; Grandma said the angels had delivered them. Gifts received were practical: pajamas, homemade mittens, or long brown stockings, except for one special present. I was seven in 1944. Many families struggled because it was wartime, World War II. I wish I had more information about what sacrifices my parents and grandparents experienced.

I was handed a package, most likely unwrapped or wrapped in brown paper because of paper shortages. I lifted the cover off the box and was in awe of a beautiful doll with closed eyes. I reached in, picked her up and her sleepy eyes opened. I laid her back down, eyes shut; picked her up, eyes opened. "I love her. I will name her, Susie." My sister, Susan, had been born in June of that year. The doll was a Horsman doll, the Horsman Company a premier doll manufacturing company in the United States at that time.

The second-favorite gift I received as a child was a doctor's kit. It was the size of a cigar box, constructed of sturdy cardboard with a metal clasp, and filled with a play watch, a thermometer, a bottle of pills (brightly colored candies), a crudely made stethoscope, and reflex hammer. I reached for the headband, inscribed Doctor, and placed it on my head. My path to a nursing career started that Christmas morning. In months to follow, my doll, Susie, or my siblings, became my patients. In the summer when I visited the farm, Grampa would let me use the empty corncrib for a make-believe hospital. Then the farm cats became patients if I could catch them.

My memory is waking up on Christmas morning and seeing the long brown stockings we hung, bulging at the bottom. The stockings usually were filled with an orange, an apple, peanuts in the shell, an assortment of Christmas candy, and a small gift such as a yoyo, coloring book, or a handheld puzzle game. As I did online research to spark my memory of Christmas in the 40s, I learned that putting an orange in a stocking represented a gift of gold from St. Nicholas.

Christmas was special to me. I didn't receive numerous gifts, but the gifts I received were remembered.

Acquired Gifts

Do you ever reflect on yourself and why you are the person you are? Genetics is a factor, but did a parent, grandparent, teacher, or babysitter influence you?

I was under the age of ten. I was wearing bib overalls, my hair in pigtails, and sitting under an oak tree at the farm, making mud pies. Grandma sat in a chair next to me knitting.

I noticed a spider crawling toward me. Grandma must have noticed it as well, because, as I was about to swat the spider, she grasped my raised hand.

"What did that spider do to you?" she asked.

"Nothing."

"That is a daddy-long-legs spider. He eats insects. As you grow up, try and find the good in people and things."

Little did she know how that incident would influence my life, but maybe she did. The word *hate* is not in my vocabulary, and I will relocate a spider from house to outside. It's not always easy to find something good in everyone so I really look and I might see beautiful blue eyes, earned aging lines in a face, or a dimple.

As I mentioned earlier in my story, Grandma also gifted me with the love of gardening as she took me by the hand and introduced her flowers by name. My story concludes as I take you, my readers, on a morning stroll through my garden, a full-circle moment with Grandma's spirit beside me.

My Sanctuary

I hold my favorite glazed pottery coffee cup in one hand, and open the front door with the other. A soft breeze caresses my face, and a temperature of 65 degrees is pleasant relief after a recent record-breaking heat wave. Viewing my gardens is a daily ritual, rain or shine. I observe change every day: new life emerging through the soil, a blossom unfurling, or a plant telling me they are not doing well and need to relocate.

Much like family, plants may flourish or struggle. When they struggle, it's time for tender-loving care. Attracting bees, butterflies, and birds is the ultimate reward of gardening.

Come with me and tour my garden sanctuary, my psychiatrist's couch so to speak. I scatter my worries amongst the flowers, hoping they germinate into solutions. The loud jeer of a bluejay welcomes morning. Birds are assembling on the near-by sandbank willow and boxelder branches, anticipating my husband's replenishing the bird feeders and filling the birdbaths. A downy woodpecker savors a breakfast of suet, while Mr. Cardinal perches on the tray feeder, cracking and eating, one by one, any leftover sunflower seeds from the previous day. Gray squirrel and a pair of mourning doves appreciate tidbits of suet dropped from above.

I start my morning stroll and stop at a corner accent garden. The branches of yellow popcorn cassia curve in the breeze beckoning me to come closer; filtered sunlight highlights pink and purple petunias at her feet. Compact Bobo hydrangea, not to be outdone, boasts many blossoms, and the branches of a waist-high conifer remind me of a ballerina's tutu.

As I pass a newly planted swamp oak, five to six feet tall, it seems to say, "Look at me. I think I've grown an inch and I'm getting more leaves." I pat his trunk in agreement. Two brown squirrels race across the lawn one in pursuit of the other, in and out of flower beds, and down the path into the woods.

I stop to view hostas planted beneath a stretch of sandbank willow: Humpback Whale, Paradigm, and Fragrant Dream. Purple and red verbena give a pop of color to the shady area.

Fond memories come to mind as I pass our fifty-year-old birdbath. It's about a foot high and belonged to my dad. It's used not only by the birds but by squirrels, fox, raccoon, and deer. One day, I observed a squirrel draped across the birdbath. *He must be dead.* Not dead—just enjoying his "kiddie pool."

The west garden has a backdrop of a 24-foot-wide wooden lattice fence. Every season of this garden bed and the others has its own identity. Now in August, most perennials are taller, bushier, with dominant colors of yellow, red, and purple. Monarda's deep red summer blooms, now looking like frayed skirts, seem to say, "I've put on a show all summer—now it's time to rest."

As I continue on I see Southern Comfort huechera, stonecrop sedum, and black-eyed Susan still showing off. Becky Shasta daisy is trying to hang on, 1-2-3-4-5-6-7 blossoms. Mrs. White Delphinium has decided to rebloom and Goldenrod is ready to burst its buttons. Goldenrod, dwarf variety, is six feet tall. Oops—catalog misinformation or abundant sun this year?

Chickens can be heard cackling in the neighboring yard. Birds join in. I set my coffee cup on the ground, reach into my pocket for my cell phone and turn on the Merlin bird app. It identifies a house finch, chipping sparrow, catbird, and a crow; all announcing morning has broken.

I've reached the south garden. In the spring, daffodils and peonies adorn this bed. Now pink and white phlox, blue *Platycodon* (balloon flowers), purple hyssop, and daylilies grace the area. Fran Hals daylily is proud of his last three blooms of the season and should be. The rusty crimson petals with yellow stripes are awesome. This handsome first bicolor daylily is named after a Dutch Golden Age painter 1582-1666.

A hand-painted bench—lucky garage sale find, gifted to me by my daughter, Julie—invites me to sit down, finish my coffee, and do nothing but enjoy. I am surrounded by spirea, senna, and Aphrodite *Calycanthus* shrub. The shrub displays big glossy leaves, but a few months ago, it exploded with enormous, deep red magenta cupped fragrant flowers.

After finishing my coffee, I rise and continue on my garden journey, passing the gazebo bordered by *Platycodon, Echinacea* (coneflowers), and *Helianthus* (false sunflower).

As I walk across the patio, roses whisper for me to visit. They should know by now no tree, shrub, or plant is ignored. At the front of the rose bed is a fairy and gnome garden, the figurines often rearranged by squirrels, rabbits, or a groundhog. I kneel and put things back where I think they should be.

I welcome walking out of the sun into the shade garden, where twenty-six varieties of hosta are intermixed with ferns, spring-blooming bleeding hearts, *Hakonechloa* (Japanese grass), solomon seal, epimedium, dwarf goatsbeard, and *Alchemilla* mollis (lady's mantle).

I open the chain-link gate and walk on the mulch path into an oasis of sorts. In the spring of 2022, I transformed the backyard into a no-yard. Before I began the project, my concern was how to get rid of the grass since I'm a non-user of weed-killers, insecticides, and pesticides. A reliable source said in this case, Round-up was acceptable, as it was more advantageous to leave the grass roots intact rather than disturbing the soil. The grass died in about a week after application of

Round-up, several inches of mulch were applied, and planting began. (There are several categories of Round-up. Choose the one for your situation).

Two hundred and forty concrete edger bricks, weighing ten pounds each, were transported twelve at a time by wheelbarrow to the backyard by my husband and me.

On hands and knees, I arranged each one to define areas, and then spread nine yards of mulch on the paths and garden beds. The focal point of the center garden is "Magnolia Jane," planted in memory of our daughter, Mary, who died in a car accident in 2018. It's surrounded by pollinator-attracting shrubs and perennials, namely "Pucker Up" dogwood, "Vanilla Spice" sweetshrub, winterberry, specialty conifers, baptisia, and lavender. The outer beds are abundantly filled with iris, daylilies, hibiscus, phlox, clematis, hollyhocks, and spring-flowering bulbs. Viburnum, Eastern cedar, hydrangea, and European Larch add form. A concrete bench, blue ceramic birdbath, and a statue of St. Francis adorn the area.

I sit down in a strategically placed lawn chair with a view. I reflect on the beauty around me, and am amazed how lush the flowers and shrubs are because of an abundance of sunshine this summer and prudent watering. I watch bumble-

bees flit from blossom to blossom of the lavender and the delightfully fragrant foliage of *Calamintha nepeta*. I file these glimpses away in my cranial memory box, ready for me to retrieve on a wintery day.

A sadness comes over me with summer's end approaching, and then I remind myself of the wintery beauty that lies ahead. Seed heads will provide a treat for the birds, fresh snow will blanket the shrubs, and the vibrant red winterberry will look like a Christmas tree adorned with miniature red bulbs.

Gardening does not end with winter; it's a new beginning as I will ponder over garden catalogs in search of a plant or shrub I may have heard about from a friend, at a garden lecture or tour. A gardener's motto is: *Always room for one more,* which means a garden is always in transition: adding, transplanting, removing, dividing, mulching, weeding, but most of all—enjoying.

My garden stimulates all my senses: the softness of the European Larch or firmness of sedum; visually the color, shape, and movement of plants; the fragrance of Hansa shrub rose and lily of the valley; the taste of daylilies or nasturtiums; and the sounds of bees, birds, frogs, and crickets.

I thank my grandmother for taking me by the hand so long ago and introducing her flowers to me *by name.*

A Tattered House and Barn Full of Memories.

The photo below shows my great-grandson, Eren, and me taking one last look. Eren is sixth generation. Photos of the farm were taken in August 2024. The current owners of the property hope to restore the house.

Acknowledgements

I extend warm thanks to my sister, Patricia, for asking me to write my memories of our maternal grandparents' farm. It has been a pleasant journey.

I appreciate feedback I received from Laurie Scheer, facilitator of the Wisconsin Writer's Association Non-fiction and Fiction Critique Group, and fellow classmates Susan Cushing, Joan Downs, Thekla Fagerlie-Madsen, Deborah Farris, Valerie Gibbons, Elgin Hushbeck, Nancy Jorgensen, Rosie Klepper, Jim Landwehr, Jeffrey Lewis, Alex Newman, Naomi Yaeger, and Julie Zachman .

I thank Rose Clark, archivist at the Juneau County Historical Museum, for taking the time to sit with me and sift through the record books.

Sincere thanks to Jerry Apps, award-winning and renowned author of many books about rural history and country life, for reviewing my essays and writing the Foreword. I'm honored.

I thank my choir member friend, Joan Schultz, for taking the time to read my manuscript and writing a review.

My writer's journey would not be possible without the support of my husband, Mike, and my publisher, Kira Henschel.

* * *

I have written my memories and my stories and am the oldest of seven children. My siblings are Mary, Fred, Susan, Barbara (deceased), Rita, and Patricia. When Grandma Debovik passed, I was ten, Mary was seven, Fred six, Susan, three, and Barbara, seven months. Rita and Patricia were born later.

Mary and Fred, as young as they were, had their own special memories. I thank them for sharing.

Mary: Amazing, vivid, childhood memories of my grandparents' farm linger eighty years later—the crunch of snow, pump water, pollywogs, saltlicks, trolls in the silo, hay stacks, a play farm set, the *Timbertoe* book, mud pies, Grandma's rye bread and potato pancakes, and a green calico dress made from a flour sack. I think childhood memories are so real because back then you truly lived in the moment.

Fred: I remember trout swimming between the milk cans in the Spring Creek milk house.

I remember homemade rye bread and churned butter.

I remember people crying in the house when World War II ended.

I remember standing guard in the oat field to hit mice with a small pitchfork at threshing time.

And Sis, I remember taking cooked cow tongue out of my lunch bucket and putting it in yours because I didn't like it.

May angels always be with you
on your life's journey.

About the Author

Rose Bingham is a retired registered nurse. She graduated from St. Francis School of Nursing in LaCrosse, Wisconsin in 1958, and received her BSN from the University of Wisconsin in Madison in 1996. She enjoys writing poetry and has been recognized for such at the annual Writer's Conference in Madison, Wisconsin in 2013, 2014, and 2015, with one of the poems published in the *Midwest Review 4*, a literary and arts magazine published by the University of Wisconsin-Madison Division of Continuing Studies. She has had published submissions in *Creative Wisconsin* magazine. Her memoir, *Buy The Little Ones a Dolly*, was published in December 2017, an inspirational, *Say It Isn't So And Then Make Lemon*ade in July 2019, and prose and poetry, *Life Through My Eyes* in 2022 by HenschelHaus Publishing. She hopes her readers will enjoy her memoir, *Yesterday's Child*. Her current project is a romance novel.

Rose is proud of her status as mother, grandmother, and great-grandmother. Rose resides in Reedsburg, Wisconsin with her husband, Mike.

May angels always be with you
on your life's journey

www.ingramcontent.com/pod-product-compliance
Lightning Source LLC
Chambersburg PA
CBHW050819090426
42737CB00021B/3446